Famous & From Missouri, U.S.A.

By: Cynthia Martin

Famous & From
Missouri, U.S.A.

By: Cynthia Martin

Windy Hills
Publishing

<u>Famous & From</u>

<u>Missouri, U.S.A.</u>

By: Cynthia Martin

To my family, friends
and students,
THANK YOU!
Thank you for your
excitement and
encouragement.
You are all awesome!

Library of Congress Cataloging-in-Publication Date is available

ISBN: 979-8-9864419-0-0 (ebook)
ISBN: 979-8-9864419-1-7 (hardcover)
ISBN: 979-8-9864419-2-4 (Paperback)

Printed in the United States of America

10 9 8 7 6 5 4 3 2

First Edition 2024

Edited by Carla Taylor
Book Cover and Illustrations by Cynthia Martin
Published by Windy Hills Publishing

Windy Hills Publishing

www.windyhillspublishing.com

Famous & From

Table of Contents

Famous and From Missouri

Famous and From Missouri is a compilation of short biographies of famous, native Missourians. It's a great quick glance at just a few of the famous, amazing and inspiring individuals from the great state. Each Missourian is categorized by one of the famous things for which they were known.

Red words will appear throughout the book. These words will have definitions to help you understand their meaning. Those definitions will be located in the glossary.

Who is your favorite Missourian?

Can you think of any people to add? Remember they need to be a native Missourian.

Thank you for taking time to learn more about the amazing people from Missouri. Enjoy!

Missouri, U.S.A.

Missouri is located in the midwest and center of the United State of America *a.k.a.* North America.

Facts about Missouri:

24th State to Join Union ~ August 10, 1821

Capital ~ Jefferson City

18th most Populated State in 2021

State Symbols:

Bird: Bluebird

Animal: Missouri Mule

Tree: Flowering Dogwood

Fish: Channel CatFish

Major League Sports

Kansas City:
Royals (Baseball)
Chiefs (Football)
Sporting KC (Soccer)

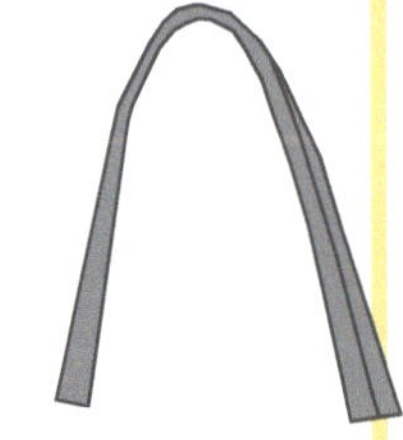

Saint Louis:
St. Louis Cardinals (Baseball)
St. Louis Blues (Ice Hockey)
St. Louis City SC (Soccer)

Known for
Kansas City Barbeque
Lewis and Clark Trail
The Saint Louis Arch

Famous Actors, Actresses and Comedians from Missouri

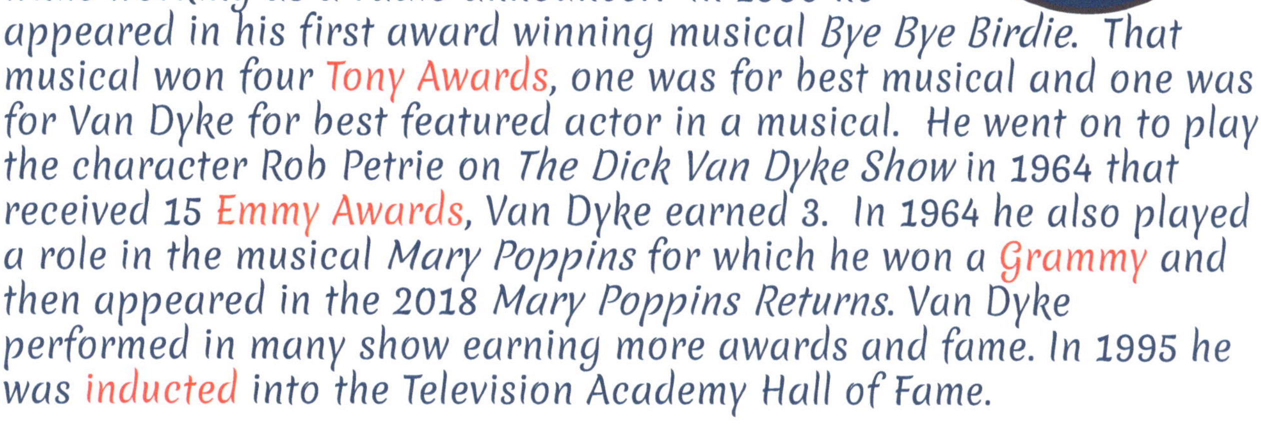

Dick Van Dyke
Actor and Comedian
1925~ Present
Born : West Plains, Missouri

Richard (Dick) Van Dyke was born in West Plains, Missouri but grew up spending most of his years in Illinois. He served in World War II while working as a radio announcer. In 1960 he appeared in his first award winning musical *Bye Bye Birdie*. That musical won four Tony Awards, one was for best musical and one was for Van Dyke for best featured actor in a musical. He went on to play the character Rob Petrie on *The Dick Van Dyke Show* in 1964 that received 15 Emmy Awards, Van Dyke earned 3. In 1964 he also played a role in the musical *Mary Poppins* for which he won a Grammy and then appeared in the 2018 *Mary Poppins Returns*. Van Dyke performed in many show earning more awards and fame. In 1995 he was inducted into the Television Academy Hall of Fame.

Redd Foxx
Actor and Comedian
1922 ~ 1991
Born : St. Louis, Missouri

Redd Foxx is known for his adult comedy and appearances on various television series. While he was well known for his time on *Sanford and Son* and *The Redd Foxx Comedy Hour (Foxx Show)* he is most known for his influence within comedy.

John Goodman
Actor
1952 ~ Present
Born : Affton, Missouri

John Goodman attended Southwest Missouri State University and after graduating in 1975 he moved to New York. He started with acting roles in small dinner theatres. Then he began adding television commercials and had a part in a Broadway production when he began his career on *Roseanne*. While working on the hit television series he earned 7 Emmy Award nominations and a Golden Globe Award. He has appeared in over 20 movies and is also known for his voice overs in many animated films such as *Monsters University*.

Edie McClurg
Actress and Comedian
1951 ~ Present
Born : Kansas City, Missouri

Edie McClurg has appeared or done a voice over in over 100 films and television programs. Some of them include, <u>The David Letterman Show</u>, <u>A River Runs Through It</u>, <u>Ferris Bueller's Day Off</u>, <u>Little Mermaid</u> and <u>Frozen.</u>

Phyllis Smith
Actress
1951~ Present
Born : St. Louis, Missouri

Phyllis Smith was awarded the Screen Actors Guild Award for Outstanding Performance by an Ensemble in a Comedy. She has appeared and done voice overs in a number of movies and television shows. Some of her shows includes, *The Office, Inside Out, Bad Teacher, Alvin* and *The Chipmunks* and *The OA*.

Famous Athletes from Missouri

Yogi Berra
Baseball Player, Catcher, Manager and Coach
1925 ~ 2015
Born : St. Louis, Missouri

Lawrence Peter Berra received the nickname Yogi in his teen years. He spent most of his baseball career with the New York Yankees baseball team. He was elected into the Hall of Fame in 1972. He was also a 10 time World Series Champion, a 15-Time All Star and a 3 time American League MVP Award winner.

Candace Parker
Basketball Player
1986~ Present
Born: St. Louis, Missouri

Being a former NBA player is only one of the many accomplishments of Candace Parker. She is a two-time Gold medalist with Team USA, won a variety of championships and is the first documented female to slam dunk in a game in the state of Illinois.

Steve Rogers
MLB Pitcher
1949 ~ Present
Born: Jefferson City, Missouri

Stephen Rogers is a 5 time All -Star right handed pitcher who played with the Montreal Expos.

Rusty Wallace
Race Car Driver
1956 ~ Present
Born : St. Louis, Missouri

      Rusty Wallace has been involved in racing for over 40 years, not only as a race car driver and champion but also as an announcer. He won the 1989 NASCAR Cup Series and currently has the third longest winning streak in history. He is a member of the NASCAR Hall of Fame, along with other National and International Motorsports Hall of Fames. He has also been recognized as a broadcaster and an *analyst*. Along with his racing he has a career in public speaking, does charity work and is the principal stakeholder in the Rusty Wallace Automotive Group dealerships in Tennessee.

Leon Spinks
Boxer
1953 ~ 2021
Born: St. Louis, Missouri

     Leon Spinks was a professional boxer who won the Heavyweight Championship in 1987 when he defeated Muhammad Ali in a split decision.

Tom Watson
Golfer
1949 ~ Present
Born : Kansas City,Missouri

     Tom Watson made his *debut* in 1975. Over his golfing career he has won 2 Masters, 14 Champion Tours and 8 Major championships along with 39 PGA Tour wins.

Famous Authors and Artist from Missouri

Maya Angelou
Author and Poet
1928 ~ 2014
Born : St. Louis,
Missouri

Maya was born with the name of Marguerite Annie Johnson. While being a native of Missouri she spent most of her childhood years in Arkansas. Her difficult childhood lead her to write many autobiographical works. Her first published work in 1969, was made into a movie in 1979 and earned her a nomination for the National Book Award. She went on to win other awards for her various works including a Tony in 1997, a Grammy in 1993, 1995, and 2002, and in 2011 was awarded the Presidential Medal of Freedom. Among her many achievements she was also the first African American woman to have a feature film produced off her screenplay.

Dale Carnegie
Inspirational Author
1888 ~ 1955
Born : Maryville, Missouri

Even though Dale Carnegie discussed many topics he is best known for his self-improvement and interpersonal skill lectures and books. His most famous book is *How to Win Friends and Influence People*.

Samuel Clemens
Author
1835 ~ 1910
Born : Florida ,Missouri

Samuel Clemens had many occupations a few were a store keeper, an artist for his brother's paper and a justice of the peace. The occupation we know him most for is his writings. He wrote in several pen names but is best known from his pseudonym name Mark Twain.

Mary Engelbreit
Artist
1952 ~ Present
Born: St. Louis, Missouri

At 11 Mary and her Mother converted an old closet into an art studio. Over the years she developed her own style and after high school began working at an art supply store. From there she went to work at a small ad agency. However, it wasn't until after taking her portfolio to a publishing house in New York for books and being told to try greeting cards did Mary really begin to focus on her talent on cards. Her cards became so well known that they got the attention of others looking to use her artwork. She has had her artwork displayed on around 6,500 products and had her own magazine _Mary Engelbreit's Home Companion_.

Joyce Meyer
Inspirational Author and Evangelist
1943 ~ Present
Born : St. Louis ,Missouri

Joyce Meyer is a New York Times bestselling author. She has written over 130 books in 155 different languages. Her books discuss some of the struggles in her own life and how her personal relationship with God has helped her through. Her writing is geared to help others do the same.

Famous Historical Figures and Outlaws from Missouri

Thomas Horn, Jr.
Outlaw and Scout
1860 ~ 1903
Born : Scotland County, Missouri

Tom Horn was the fifth child in a family of 12 kids and had a difficult childhood. At 16 he left home and became a scout for the U.S. Cavalry. During that time he was part of many fights and wars. He was also known for his range detective and tracking skills. He wrote an autobiography about his life while in jail for one of the killings committed possibly while being a hired gunman.   His life has been made into various television shows and movies.

Jesse James
American 'Outlaw'
1847 ~ 1882
Born: Clay County, Missouri (Near Present day Kearney)

Jesse James was known as a bank and train robber as well as the leader of the James-Younger gang.

Calamity Jane
American Frontiersman
1852 ~ 1903
Born : Princeton, Missouri

Martha Jane Cannary was the oldest of six. At the age of 12 she found herself raising these siblings when both parents had passed away. In 1895 she joined Buffalo Bill's Wild West Show. There she became known for her sharpshooting and horse riding skills.

<u>Myra Maybelle Shirley Reed Starr</u>
American 'Outlaw'
1848 ~ 1889
Born : Carthage, Missouri

Myra Maybelle became known as Belle Starr. In 1863 following the burning of Carthage her family moved to Texas. She had ties with the Younger Brothers as well as Jesse and Frank James. Her home in Texas was often the gangs' refuge. Over the years she became known as an outlaw known for robbery and stealing horses.

Younger Brothers
American 'Outlaws'
Born : Lee Summit, Missouri

The Younger Brothers were Cole 1844 - 1916, John 1846 - 1874, James (Jim) 1850 - 1902, Robert (Bob) 1853 - 1889. Their gang also consisted of Jesse James and Joseph McCarty who was Billy the Kid's brother. When the brothers were young they witnessed fighting and war. As they got older they joined in on confederate raids and formed their own gang. Their gang was known for robbing banks and trains in Missouri and surrounding states. Over the years some were shot or injured during robberies and escapes. Three of the gang members plead guilty to robbery and murder and were sentenced to life in prison. One brother died due to illness while imprisoned. The other two of the remaining brothers received pardons in 1901.

Famous Musicians from Missouri

Aaron Dontez Yates
Rapper, Songwriter, Actor
1971 ~ Present
Born : Kansas City, Missouri

Aaron Dontez Yates a.k.a. Tech N9ne is known for his music but also for being one of the founders of the music label Strange Music. His rapping style is classified as a rhyming chopper style rap.

Joseph Vernon Turner Jr.
Musician
1911 ~ 1985
Born : Kansas City, Missouri

Joseph Turner was also known as "Big Joe." He began his musical career singing in church choirs. Later he began singing in local K.C. bars until discovered then moved to New York. In New York he sang in various nightclubs and in 1938 sang at Carnegie Hall. Soon he was recording with top jazz musicians. By 1950 he was known from his rock and roll recordings such as "Shake, Rattle and Roll," however many of his hits were sung by others. He also appeared in movies, television, festivals and jazz clubs. In 1983 he was inducted into the Blues Hall of Fame and 1987 into the Rock and Roll Hall of Fame.

Chuck Berry
Musician
1926 ~ 2017
Born : St. Louis, Missouri

Chuck was known as a singer and songwriter. He was also influential in the rhythm and blues and rock and roll genres during the 1950's - 1970's. He won a Grammy in 1984 and in 1998 was inducted into the Rock and Roll Hall of Fame.

Marshall Bruce Mathers III
Singer, Songwriter
1972 ~ Present
Born : St. Joseph, Missouri

Marshall is well known as Eminem or by his rapping *persona* Slim Shady. He was one of the best-selling and controversial artist in the mid to late 1990's and early 2000's. He had a rough childhood and by the age of 14 he was rapping in clubs in Detroit, Michigan. He caught the eye of Dr. Dre after placing second in the Freestyle category at Rap Olympics. Dr. Dre later became his producer and mentor. He has also won two Grammy Awards and four *MTV* awards for his music videos.

Sheryl Crow
Singer, Songwriter
1962 ~ Present
Born : Kennett, Missouri

Growing up around music Sheryl found herself playing the piano at 5 years old. By high school she could play by ear, composed her first song, and played the guitar in various local rock bands. The first few years after college she taught music to special needs children. In 1986 she moved to Los Angeles, California. Once there she was able to continue her journey in the music industry. She toured with many famous bands including touring with Michael Jackson for two years. Then she worked as a backup singer for various bands such as Stevie Wonder, Rod Stewart and Sting. Her compositions were also being recorded by well known artist like Eric Clapton. About this time she had released her first album which won three Grammy Awards: best record, best pop vocal performance and best new artist. In 1996 she won two more *Grammys* on her second album, best rock album and best vocal performance.

Famous Presidents, Political Figures, and Journalist From Missouri

Walter Cronkite Jr.
Journalist, Anchor
1916 ~ 2009
Born : St. Joseph, Missouri

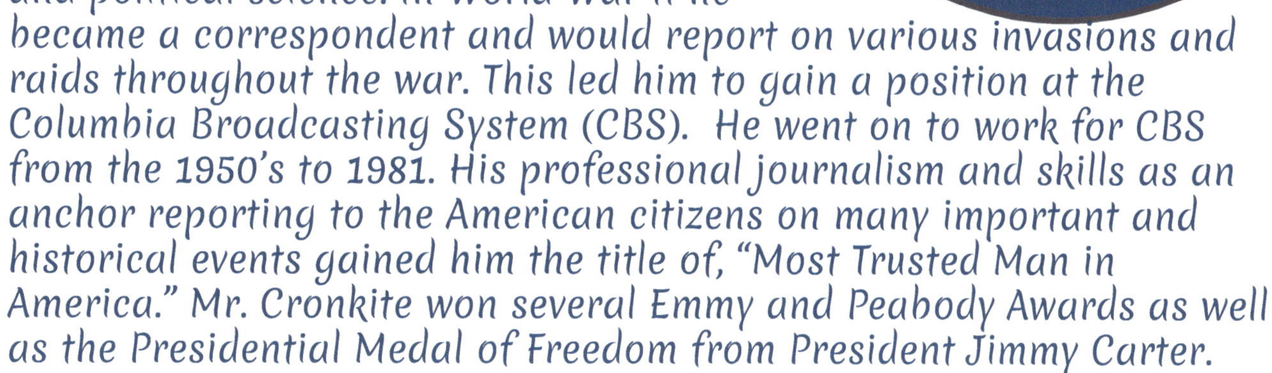

Walter Cronkite Jr. grew up with a love for reading, journalism and political science. In World War II he became a correspondent and would report on various invasions and raids throughout the war. This led him to gain a position at the Columbia Broadcasting System (CBS). He went on to work for CBS from the 1950's to 1981. His professional journalism and skills as an anchor reporting to the American citizens on many important and historical events gained him the title of, "Most Trusted Man in America." Mr. Cronkite won several Emmy and Peabody Awards as well as the Presidential Medal of Freedom from President Jimmy Carter.

Rush Limbaugh III
Political Commentator, Radio Personality and Author
1951 ~ 2021
Born : Cape Girardeau, Missouri

Rush Limbaugh is known mostly for his political views that he would discuss throughout his life. He began his radio career at 16 working for his local station. From there he worked in various cities at their stations as a commentator. His show The Rush Limbaugh Show debuted in 1988. He was considered an important part of the Republican Party and received the Presidential Medal of Freedom in 2020.

John J. Pershing
United States General
1860 ~ 1948
Born : Laclede, Missouri

John J. Pershing is most known for being a U.S. Army General during World War One (WWI). He graduated from West Point a military academy in 1886. After graduating he was assigned as second lieutenant to the 6th Cavalry. In 1891 he was living in Lincoln, Nebraska as an instructor in military science while earning a law degree. In 1897 he returned to West Point as a tactics instructor. He was involved in many battles and wars including the Spanish-American War, the Marco Rebellion and WWI. Through his time leading his troops he became known as "Black Jack".

Harry S. Truman
President
1884 ~ 1972
Born : Lamar, Missouri

Harry S. Truman was the oldest of three and graduated high school from Independence, Missouri. After graduating he worked as a bank clerk in Kansas City. He volunteered in WWI. He volunteered two tours in 1905 -1911 with the National Guard then again during WWI and fought in France. He returned to the United States in 1919 and married his childhood friend Elizabeth (Bess) Wallace. After the war he became a county Judge serving two, four year terms for a total of eight years. In 1945 Truman ran as the Democratic Vice President for Roosevelt who became the president that year. However, Roosevelt passed away the following April. This made Truman the 33rd president of the United States of America. He held office for the last months of WWII and during the beginning of the Cold War. He served two terms as president from 1945 - 1953.

Famous Scientists and Inventors from Missouri

Susan Blow
Creator, Author and Lecturer
1843 ~ 1916
<u>Born</u> : Carondelet, ,Missouri (Present day St. Louis)

Susan is know for taking her knowledge of education and helping to create what we now know as Kindergarten. In 1870 she traveled to Germany and became interested in their revolutionary ideas of kindergarten. She went on to create the first public kindergarten in the United State in 1873 which was established in St. Louis. In the following years she trained many teachers, wrote several books and began lecturing at a teachers college.

George Washington Carver
Scientist
1860's - 1943
<u>Born</u> : Diamond Grove, Missouri

George Carver was born into slavery but in 1865 the abolition of slavery gave him freedom. While working to obtain his high school education he worked as a farmhand. He became an American Agricultural chemist who helped to revolutionize agriculture and produce over 500 different shades of dyes that were imported from Europe before World War II.

Jack Dorsey
CEO and Founder
1976 - Present
Born : St. Louis, Missouri

Jack Dorsey is known as a entrepreneur and philanthropist as well as being a billionaire. However, he is most known as a Co-founder and CEO of Twitter and Founder and CEO of Square, a financial company. In 2012 The Wall Street Journal gave him Innovator of the Year award.

Edwin Hubble
Teacher, Astronomer
1889 -1953
Born : Marshfield, Missouri

Edwin Hubble discovered that there were comparable distant galaxies beyond our own. He has earned many awards over his lifetime from the years of 1924 - 1946. The Hubble Space Telescope was named after him and has allowed us a greater glimpse of the universe.

Norbert Wiener
Scientist and Inventor of Cybernetics
1894 -1964
Born : Columbia, Missouri

Norbert Wiener was a mathematician and philosopher but is known as the father or inventor of Cybernetics. He described cybernetics as "the study of control and communication in the animal and the machine".

 Glossary

A.K.A. ~ Also Known As another name by which something goes by

Analyst ~ A job where one examines the relationship of something

Astronomer ~ Is a scientist that studies things beyond Earth, such as galaxies, moons, planets and the stars.

Autobiographical (Autobiography) ~ The account or telling of one's own life

Categorize ~ To put in to a category by sorting

CEO ~ Is a person with the Chief Executive decision making authority in an Organization or business

Commentator ~ A person who provides or reports, news, sport events or other similar things broadcasted.

Compilation ~ A gathering of materials or documents into a collection

Debut :(debuted) ~ The first appearance

Democrat ~ Is a member of the Democratic Party in the U.S. politics

Emmy Awards ~ An annual award for outstanding achievement or excellence in television

Ensemble ~ A group of (musicians, actors, items etc.) together create an ensemble

Founder ~ Someone that begins, starts or establishes something

Golden Globe Award ~ An annual award ceremony held to award outstanding achievement or excellence in television and motion pictures

Grammy Award ~ A series of annual awards for those in the music industry to recognize their achievement within the industry according to the musics genres

Glossary Continued

Inducted ~ To formally become a specific position, title or organization

MTV ~ A cable channel that focused on music related programs geared towards America's young adults.

Native ~ To be born or reside in a specific place, a local resident

National Book Award ~ An annual award given to, "celebrate the best literature in America…"

Nominations ~ To be picked or selected for a position, award or group (Nominations for president would be those that we are voting on)

Presidential Medal of Freedom ~ A medal bestowed by the President to recognize people that have made a great contribution

Persona ~ A character or role one displays in public.

Philosopher ~ A person that studies and seeks a greater understanding of life, what makes us how we are, a greater understanding of the world around us, wisdom, ethics, relationships, or enlightenment

Pseudonym ~ A made up name, also known as a pen name it is common for authors to use instead of their real names

Red ~ Primary color next to orange on the color spectrum and opposite violet. Red like cherries, Red like fire, Red like rubies

Refuge ~ A building or place one may go for safety or shelter.

Republican Party ~ A political Party in the U.S. a member of this political party is known as a Republican

Rock and Roll Hall of Fame ~ Museum is located in Cleveland, Ohio in the U.S.

Tony Award ~ Is award, annually given to recognize the best live performances in the Broadway theatres. The ceremony takes place in Midtown Manhattan, New York and is presented by the The Broadway League and American Theatre Wing.

<u>Create Your Own Famous &</u>
<u>From</u>

____

____
(Occupation)

__________ **~ Present**
(Year you were born)

<u>**Born :** __________ , __________</u>

Write about yourself below

____

____

____

____

____

____

References

Websites:

"Hall of Fame Explorer - Baseballhall.org." National Baseball Hall of Fame.Spring 2021{https://baseballhall.org/}

"People-Biography.com." Biography. Accessed Spring 2021 {https://www.biography.com}

Encyclopaedia Britannica. Accessed Spring 2021 {https://www.britannica.com}

"About Candace." Candace Parker. Accessed Spring 2021 {https://candaceparker.com/}

"About Us." Joyce Meyer Ministries. Accessed Spring 2021 {https://joycemeyer.org}

"Meet Mary." Mary Engelbreit. Accessed Spring 2021 {https://www.maryengelbreit.com}

"Players." MLB. Accessed Spring 2021 {https://www.mlb.com}

"Learn About Missouri." Mo.gov. Accessed Spring 2021 {https://www.mo.gov/education/learn-about-missouri/}

"Start Search." P.B.S. Accessed Spring 2021 {https://pbs.org}

"About Rusty Wallace." Rusty Wallace. Accessed Spring 2021 {https://rustywallace.com}

"History Truman." Missouri Secretary of State. Accessed Spring 2021 {https://www.sos.mo.gov}

"About Tom". Tom Waston. Accessed Spring 2021 {https://tomwatson.com}

Thank you for reading!

Famous and From Missouri

Famous and From gives the reader a quick glimpse of various famous people from Missouri. These famous Missourians were all born in the State of Missouri and have been sorted by one of the things that made them famous. The categories span from Actors/Actress, Outlaws to Scientists, and many more. It might surprise you to see some of the famous Missourians from the past to present day. Join us in learning more about the wonderful people of Missouri and see if we included your favorite Missourian.

Meet the Author

Cynthia's love and enjoyment for reading and writing has grown stronger through her life. It began when she was young reading with her Mother and Grandparents and continued through her professional educational years and personal life: teaching, parenting, becoming a librarian and published author.

She has overcome her own reading difficulties and struggles when younger and seeks to help all those she can to enjoy the pleasure of reading a good book and becoming a lifelong lover of life and learning. Some of her children's books share her positive and encouraging lifestyles, while others gives glimpse into the knowledge she has learned.

www.ingramcontent.com/pod-product-compliance
Lightning Source LLC
Chambersburg PA
CBHW041648110726
48005CB00003B/750